Firefighters

Izzi Howell

W
FRANKLIN WATTS
LONDON • SYDNEY

Franklin Watts
First published in Great Britain in 2018 by The Watts Publishing Group
Copyright © The Watts Publishing Group, 2018

Produced for Franklin Watts by
White-Thomson Publishing Ltd
www.wtpub.co.uk

ISBN: 978 1 4451 6489 2
10 9 8 7 6 5 4 3 2 1

Credits
Series Editor: Izzi Howell
Series Designer: Rocket Design (East Anglia) Ltd
Designer: Clare Nicholas
Literacy Consultant: Kate Ruttle

The publisher would like to thank the following for permission to reproduce their pictures: Getty: Monty Rakusen cover, kali9 4, Monkey Business Images 8b, Martyn Goddard 9, skodonnell 10, sanchairat 12, sergeyryzhov 14l, Joel Carillet 16t, SteveAllenPhoto 17, dlewis33 19, ziggy1 20, Jupiterimages, Creatas Images 22; Shutterstock: sandyman title page and 13, TFoxFoto 5, photka 6, MZeta 7l, Plamen Galabov 7r, Christine Bird 8t, Dale A Stork 11, Phichai 14r, Dariush M 15, Fotos593 16b, Tyler Olson 18, Lec Neo 21tl, Janis Smits 21tc, Gita Kulinitch Studio 21tr, napocska 21b.
Every attempt has been made to clear copyright. Should there be any inadvertent omission please apply to the publisher for rectification.

Printed in China

Franklin Watts
An imprint of
Hachette Children's Group
Part of The Watts Publishing Group
Carmelite House
50 Victoria Embankment
London EC4Y 0DZ

An Hachette UK Company
www.hachette.co.uk
www.franklinwatts.co.uk

All words in **bold** appear in the glossary on page 23.

Contents

Who are firefighters?

Firefighters **rescue** people from fires. They put out fires to stop them from getting bigger.

Have you ever seen a firefighter? Where were you?

▲ Firefighters work together in a team.

Firefighters also rescue people from other places. They help people who are **trapped** in cars after a car accident.

▲ These firefighters are taking the doors off a car after an accident. They will help the people inside the car to get out.

Emergency!

People call the firefighters if there is a **dangerous** fire. In the UK, they ring 999 on the phone and ask for the fire service. In Australia, they call 000.

In the UK, people ring 999 in an emergency. ▶

Calling...

999

An alarm rings in the fire station when the firefighters have to go to an **emergency**. They stop what they are doing and go to the **fire engine**.

◀ Some fire stations have a pole. Firefighters quickly slide down the pole and run to the fire engine.

▼ Firefighters run to the fire engine in an emergency.

Fire engines

Everything that firefighters need in an emergency is inside the fire engine.

ladder

hoses

spare uniform

tools

rescue packs

Fire & Rescue Service

◀ Firefighters sit at the front of the fire engine.

Firefighters drive quickly to an emergency in the fire engine. The fire engine has flashing lights and a **siren**.

The fire engine's lights and siren tells other drivers to let the fire engine go in front of them.
▼

What noise does a fire engine make?

9

Uniform

helmet

radio

torch

Firefighters wear a uniform.
Their uniform **protects**
them from fire.

◀ The firefighter's thick jacket
and trousers stop the fire
from burning him.

gloves

jacket

trousers

glow in the
dark stripes

**Why do
you think
firefighters
need a torch?**

boots

If there is a lot of smoke, firefighters need help to breathe. They use an **oxygen mask**.

▲ The firefighter wears the oxygen mask over his face.

Rescuing people

When firefighters arrive at the fire, they find out if they need to rescue anyone. They go into the building to help people escape.

▲ Firefighters carry people out of the building. People can get hurt in fires.

Once everyone is safe, firefighters try to put out the fire. They don't want the fire to spread to nearby buildings.

▼ It can take a long time to put out a fire.

Equipment

Firefighters use different **equipment**. They use an axe to break through closed doors.

◀ Firefighters use a tall ladder to rescue people who are trapped high in a building.

▲ an axe

Firefighters put out fires with water. They spray water on the fire from a large **hose**.

▼ Water from the hose puts out the fire.

Trapped people

Firefighters also rescue people who are trapped. People are sometimes trapped in high places or under something heavy.

◀ **These firefighters are helping someone trapped on the roof of a building.**

These firefighters are checking to see if anyone is trapped under this building that has fallen down. ▶

▲ Firefighters use boats to help people escape from floods.

People sometimes get trapped during a **flood**. They can't leave their homes because there is too much water.

Has there ever been a flood where you live? What happened?

The fire station

▲ These firefighters are checking the equipment in the fire engine.

Firefighters stay at the fire station while they wait for an emergency call. They get their equipment and the fire engine ready for the next emergency.

Some firefighters have to sleep at the fire station. They wake up and go to help if there is a fire during the night.

▲ Firefighters cook and eat their meals together at the fire station.

Fire safety

Fire is very dangerous. Smoke alarms make a loud noise when there is a fire in the building. If you hear a smoke alarm, keep calm and leave the building.

◀ **The smoke alarms in your home should be checked every few months to make sure they are still working.**

Where are the smoke alarms in your home?

We can stop fires from happening by being careful.

Don't leave a lit candle alone. ▼

Don't play with matches or lighters.
▼

▲ Only metal pots should touch the flames on a hob.

Quiz

Test how much you remember.

Check your answers on page 24.

1 Where do firefighters sit in the fire engine?

2 Name two parts of a firefighter's uniform.

3 What do firefighters use their ladder for?

4 Why do firefighters need to rescue people from floods?

5 What do firefighters do at the fire station?

6 How do fire alarms keep us safe from fires?

Glossary

dangerous – something that could hurt you

emergency – an important or dangerous situation that people need to sort out quickly

equipment – things that are used for an activity or job

fire engine – a vehicle that firefighters drive to emergencies and that carries their equipment

flood – when a place becomes covered in water

hose – a long tube that water comes out of

oxygen mask – a mask that helps people breathe

protect – to keep someone or something safe

radio – a piece of equipment used to send and receive spoken messages

rescue – to save someone from a dangerous situation

siren – something that makes a loud sound

trapped – if someone is trapped, they can't leave a dangerous situation

Index

Answers:

1: At the front; 2: Some items include helmet, torch, gloves, jacket, trousers and radio; 3: To reach people at the top of tall buildings; 4: Sometimes there is so much water that people can't leave their houses and people might drown or get hurt in the water; 5: Prepare the fire engine, cook and eat meals and sleep; 6: They make a loud noise to warn people when there is a fire in the building.

Teaching notes:

Children who are reading Book band Gold or above should be able to enjoy this book with some independence. Other children will need more support.

Before you share the book:

- Talk about children's prior knowledge and experience of firefighters, emphasising their role in keeping people and places safe.
- Check that children have a good understanding of why fires can be dangerous.
- If any children have seen firefighters fighting a fire, invite them to share their experiences.

While you share the book:

- Help children to read some of the more unfamiliar words.

- Talk about the questions. Encourage children to make links between their own experiences and the information in the book.
- Discuss the pictures, talking about what the firefighters are doing and why. Talk about the equipment they are using.
- Do children know where the nearest fire station is?

After you have shared the book:

- If possible, take children to visit a fire station, or invite a firefighter to come and talk to the class and demonstrate some of their equipment.
- Make a poster of things explaining why fires can be dangerous.
- Work through the free activity sheets at www.hachetteschools.co.uk